Table of Contents

When the Lights Went Out

By: Earl Tillis

Manuscript – **When The Lights Went Out"** by: Earl's Tillis

INTRODUCTION:

During the many years of my life I have contemplated many things. In my youth I wondered what would I be doing in 5 years? What kind of future would I have? And Is God for real?

I knew that I was not the only one who had questions about the existence of God. I remember a time, when a girl asked this question in school, "If God is real why can't we see him? The only answer I thought of was, "wow that's a good question". With great anticipation I waited to hear the answer, knowing it was going to be a long drawn out explanation. Just as the teacher was going to attempt to give an answer the bell rang. I saw the relief on the teacher face, she was sweating bullets. That's what happens when we don't have the right answers.

Our curiosity sometimes gets the best of us. How many times did our mom tell us not to touch the stove because it was very hot!! But what did we do? We touched the stove anyway, and found out mom was right. Or we ask ourselves like the girl at school, "If God really exist why do people suffer so much? These and other questions arise when we don't know who God is.

There are a lots of times in our lives that God will give us directions that we don't understand. Like Abraham, in Genesis 12, when God told him ***"Get from your country, your people and your father's house and go to the land I will show you. 2 "I will make you into a great nation, and I will bless you; I will make your name great, and you will be a blessing".*** Abraham obeyed because he knew who God was. Just like God chose, and led Abraham, some of us sometimes wonder if God will use us? But we forget what God may require of us. God required much from Abraham, but He was with Abraham all the way.

Can you see where I am going with this? God is the creator of all things including heaven, earth, the stars, and you, and me. Like a lot of young people, when we were growing up we thought we knew everything, and no one could tell us we didn't. But as I grew older, and gained some real life experiences, now I know that I was wrong. How does the old saying go? *"If I knew then, what I know now, I would be awesome!"*

We all have experienced growing pains, some good, and some bad. The question is, **"What did we learn from it or did we learn from it?"** God continues to show us who He is, even when we don't want to learn about him, and his wonderful love for us. It is because of Him that his only son came to die for you, and me. God has a great purpose for our lives. Nobody can love you like God. Nobody can hold you or comfort you like he can. He is always right there with you. He's there in your living room, in the hospital, even in your car. He's a keeper. He is peace in the times of your storms. He's joy in the midst of your sorrow. He's your provider. **HE IS GOD!!.** You must make sure that you don't forget, that if God spoke it, he is going to make things good for you.

So I want you to come with me on this journey of faith. You may be hurting with all you are dealing with. You may be having a silent storm raging in your life. You may be in the midnight hour of certain circumstances, and you can't find anyone to talk to. Instead of you concentrating on all that has been happening to you, I want to turn the table, and have you begin to love on God. Because he's worthy to be praised, worshipped , honored

I write this book of faith for all those who have not been trusting in God, and for those who don't know who God really is. I invite you to join me on this journey of faith. I write for the person that feel that life is not worth living. I write this for the person who says, *"This is the day that I am going to give up."* But you won't give up because you're going to say to God that, *"Today I WILL trust in you".*

So let's take a step of faith, and together we will be excited about God's purpose in our lives.

All praises to God for my life, and for my family, and for all the people He has placed in my life. It is my ultimate desire that this book, and my life be an example to others, and through my testimony I dare to dream that souls may be saved.

TO GOD BE THE GLORY

Earl M, Tillis, Sr.

DEDICATION:

This book is dedicated to my wife Arcira, of many years. Throughout all these difficult times of losing my eyesight, and all of the other things I had to endure during my time of adjusting to my new set of circumstances, she was my cheerleader, my support, and my inspiration. We have continued, and even strengthened our journey of faith, and trust in God.

To my son EJ, he is my hope in difficult times. He came to my wife, and me to tell us what was on his mind, and in his heart. He said since he is the oldest of the family, that he felt he needed to drop out of college to be the supporter or provider for the family. We were so proud, and appreciative of

what he told us, but of course, we told him we didn't want him to do that. Because of our hope, and trust in God, we will make it through this. We feel you must finish what you started to complete God's promises to you.

To my youngest son Justin, who is a serious person, also a person who speaks the truth in his heart. He knows that trusting in God, knowing that in the midst of this struggle, we will make it through because of his promises to us as his children.

And to Centro de Cvida Church that started with 14 people, and now there are over 1500 members. This is a church that follows God's promises for their lives. A church that's lending their support, and prayers in my time of need.

And to my siblings, and the rest of my family, who were shocked at first at the news of me losing my eyesight, but then amazed that the will of God in being done in my life.

So this book is dedicated to all those who are an important part of my life. They are an inspiration to me, knowing that God promises of trust, faith, and hope in Christ Jesus can get you through anything.

To my oldest brother, Claude, who when I told him I could play tennis, took me out to play with some of his friends. However, for some reason, he never took me out again (inside joke). Now he helps with this book by assisting in the painstaking work of editing, He has dedicated himself to God, knowing that all things are possible through Christ who always strengthens us.

It is my hope, and prayer that this book will be an inspiration to those who have had tragic accidents, or difficult situations or experiences, aldo that others will be inspired to follow the love of Jesus Christ, and to have faith and trust in him, knowing that ***"...all things work together for the good for those who love the Lord..."*** *(Romans 8:28)* He will meet, and exceed your expectations because of his great love, and sacrifice for all of us.

Chapters 1 – The Family

This is the story of a family of struggle, deception, and many other things. I guess I want to start with my family. My family was born in the south. I used to always hear stories about my parents, and where they were born. My dad Claude R. Tillis, Sr. was born January 9, 1927 in Polkville, Mississippi, to the parents of Caley, and Willie Mae Tillis. My mom Earnestine Tillis was born August 1, 1928 in Delhi, Louisiana to the parents of George, and Clara Downs.

I don't know if you have ever heard of or know where Delhi is, but they say when you go through that town, if you blink, you'll miss it, but this is where I was born. Of the few things I know about my parent's early lives is that my father had one older brother, and my mother was the sixth child in a family of nine sister, and brothers. I never knew my grandparents, I was very young, about two years old when my parents decided to pack us all up, and move to California. I was never told nor did I ever ask why they decided to move from Louisana to California, but because we were very poor, I have to believe that it was simply to find a better life.

I was number eight in a family of nine, I had five sisters, and three brothers. I grew up knowing only two of my mom's brothers, and sisters. One was my Uncle Fuzz, I remember growing up my mom would always load us in the car, and we would go visit him often. By the way, Fuzz was not his real name, but it was the only one I knew. I learned later in life that his real name was George. You see, down in the south we often would use what we called "nick names" for each other. As a matter of fact, my grandfather gave my oldest brother the nick name "Preacher" when he was just a little boy, and the amazing thing is that when he grew up, he was called into the ministry, and now he is pastor of a church in Los Angeles. The one sister of my mom, that I remember was named Carry Bell, We all just called her Aunt Bell. I remember on time we went to her house, and we stayed up all night, just hanging out, and talking about mostly nothing, but we were together.

But me on the other hand I had to create my own world in order to cope with things, trying to figure out life on my own, After my mom, and dad separated my brother Michael, and I ended up living with my dad, where I attended Horace Mann Junior High School. God blessed me to be a pretty good athlete in a variety of sports. Nevertheless, I had a difficult time coping in those days because of gang activity in my community. You see, I went to school which was in an area controlled by the gang called "the Crips ". However, I lived in a neighborhood which was the territory of the gang called, "the Bloods". I remember one day I was playing basketball at school when some members of the Bloods came on campus, and everyone was running, but since I lived in Blood territory I knew all of them. So I had to be very, very careful not to be connected with them, because if I was, I would be in danger at the Crip school. As a matter of fact, when I look back at those times in my life, I can really see that it was a blessing that me, and my bothers, grew up at all.

There was also a time when my older brother Michael was jumped by gang members of the Crips causing him to have him punctured lungs, and broken ribs. Seemingly, there was a member of the Bloods who **"for some reason"** protected us. He even went after the Crips that had beaten Michael.

Looking back on that incident, it is clear to me that God had intervened, because he had a purpose for my life, and he blesses those whom I love. Just like he did with Abraham when he said, *And I will bless them that bless thee, and curse him that curseth thee: ....*(Genesis 12:3)

Now I am going to Crenshaw High School in Los Angeles, and I participate in multiple sports, like basketball, Tennis, and Water Polo, and I even ran track. There is an interesting story about how I joined the tennis team. One day while at school I was involved in a fight. It just so happened that the one who broke us up was the coach of the school Tennis Team. He gave me two choices, go to the Principal's office or join his tennis team. Up to now I had no interest in tennis at any time in my life, I always thought that tennis was considered a game for snobs. But seeing the better part of valor, I consented to join the school tennis team where I flourished as a team player.

Whenever I think about that time in my life, I can't help but think that this was just another time that God had intervened in my life.. I know now. that He is ever watching over us, and protecting us, and keeping us. My brother reminded me that the intervention by the tennis coach was just another time that God **was** *"working things out for the good of those who loved the Lord and are called according to his purpose".* (Romans 8;28)

Growing up, there were so many life challenges that I couldn't even imagine, because I was just a kid trying to figure it all out. It's kinda strange that when I look at the very real challenges in my young life, that in a way they don't compare to the ones in the lives of some of my older sisters, and brothers. For instance, I recall them telling me stories of how when they were very young 8,9 or 10 years old, they had to work for the family by picking cotton, and only getting $25.00 a month for

their labor. They had to work in the cotton fields from 4 or 5 o'clock in the morning until the sun went down in the evening. They had to work in the hot sun, and even in the rain.

I couldn't even imagine making $25 for one months' work,. And here I am making what I thought was big bucks when I made minimum-wage of $2.25 an hour. That was bad, but what they were forced to endure was much worse.

In my senior year, I returned to live with my mom, and graduated from Crenshaw High School in1978. After returning to live with my mom she constantly was on my back about having an one on one home Bible study. One day we were studying the passage about the Ethiopian Eunuch, who asked **"What keeps me from being baptized?"** That question rose in my heart, and I asked my teacher the same question. He responded, and asked me **"Do you want to be baptized", and** I said **"Yes".** He immediately took me down to the church, and I was baptized that same day. I remember the experience that I had, being submerge in the water, and then coming up out of that water, I screamed to the top lungs, **"I was a new child of God."**

After being baptized, I wondered what was the next step in my life but little did I know, God had it all worked out. I had found Jesus at the age of 18, and I have been baptized. I soon told my mother that I wanted to go to this Christian college in Texas. Although my parents didn't have a lot of money my mom did what she could, and paid for my transportation to Texas.

I attended SWCC, Southwestern Christian College in Terrell, Texas where I majored in Christian Studies. Because my parents couldn't pay for college, I had to apply for financial aid, and once again, God smiled on me, and I was approved. Unfortunately, it was not enough to pay for everything I

needed for school. So I got a job working on campus, and another job working off-campus at Taco Plaza to offset the cost.

As part of my Major, I took a class called "Homiletics", which is the study of sermon preparation, learning how to create sermon outlines, etc. On one occasion, I was asked to bring the message for Chapel service. I did all I could to prepare myself. I prayed, and I studied as hard as I could. I preached to the best of my ability, I extended an alter appeal, but no one responded. I was devastated, I went back to my room, and I cried like a baby. I was very disappointed in my presentation, not because of what I said or did, but because no one responded to the invitation. I felt I was doing it in God's name, and I wanted him to be proud of me. And as I was there weeping, and ask him why didn't anyone respond?, God told me, **don't worry about it, you did good, they will come when they want to come.** But know that I will always be there for you. This was a revelation that has stuck with me through my life. I realize that even though we want to do things to please God, things will always happen in his time, and not ours. That was one of the first lessons that I learned about trusting in God, and knowing that his will, will be his will. Any seed that I plant, I may not see it grow, but I know that it will one day. After doing that, I got better, and really studied hard. I realized that even in the hard times, he continues to teach me that it's about His way, not my way.

I had always been interested in playing basketball so I went out for the school basketball team. Again, God's blessings were upon me, and I made the team. I was so excited about this new journey I was on, I tried out for the school choir. I couldn't sing, but I tried out anyway, However, I wasn't accepted in the choir, but it was still an exciting opportunity for me.

After two years I left Southwest Christian College, and transferred to Washington State University to play basketball. As I walked around the Washington State campus in Pullman, Washington, I said to myself, "Look at me, I'm on the campus of a Pac-10 school". Back then I thought I was cool.

I look back, and think of where God has brought me from. I am a young black man who had little financial support from my parents but here I am at a major University. Yet still I look at God, and I am humbled by where he has led me in this stage of my life. After my time at Washington State, I returned back to California. I worked at different restaurants throughout the city. Time was passing so fast that from the age of 21 - 28 I felt like I was roaming in the wilderness because there was not anything significant happening in my life.

But I do remember going to my 10 year high school reunion which was really exciting, and different. I didn't know what to expect, but I guess that's when you see who is who. I know that through my youthful eyes back then, some of the girls were not so attractive. But now, 10 years the ones who look good to me then, do not anymore, and the ones who were unattractive then are attractive now.

One of the most impactful things I remember was there was a young man at church named Freddy, God rest his soul. We ushered together in what was called **"campaign for Christ"**, service. The very next day I found out that someone had broken into his house while he was home, and during the robbery he was shot, and killed.

When I was told about it I was devastated. I remember at his funeral service I wept like a baby, and thought to myself, **"Man, this is not right, it's not fair that someone who is living their life for Jesus Christ would lose it in such way".** At his funeral it was an open casket service, but I couldn't

bring myself to go up, and see him that way, but I learned that we have to face our fears in order to grow. This also was a part of my journey of finding Jesus, trying to live a life for Christ, and trying to do his will.

I praise God that I discovered early that I needed him in my life. With patience, and the guidance of the Lord, I met the love of my life, Arcira Escobar. We were married in January 1992. And after 27 years, we are still together today even though we have struggled with financial hard times, marital difficulties, and other family issues. This time of our lives showed our vulnerability, and favor as we chose to follow God. we had our first son, Earl, Jr. in July 1992. That same year, after the Los Angeles riots, and after the 7.2 earthquake, we decide to move to Washington State. Here I am now back in Washington the place where God showed me what was to be part of my future. Isn't it amazing how God will bring us back to where he intended us to be.

We had our second son Justin, in December 1993 while living in Federal Way, Washington. I began to think, before I was married, I only had the responsibility of taking care of myself. Now we have two boys, I was managing restaurants for a living, and I begin to wonder if I could handle the pressures of providing for my family. But, again, I realized that God is good and he is always with us.

Oh yeah, I forgot to tell you how I met my wife. I was managing a Sizzler Restaurant in Long Beach, California. Her sister Selene worked at the Sizzler that I was managing. One day Arcira came into the restaurant to visit her sister, and of course, once I saw her, as manager, it was my responsibility to greet our guest, and welcome them to the restaurant. I have to admit that this time I did it because she was so cute. As part of customer service I stopped by her table for a few minutes to see if everything was OK.

It just so happened that she barely spoke English, and I could speak very little Spanish. She would sometimes park in back of the restaurant, and one day she saw me at the back door, and thought I was the security guard. She was worried that I would tell her to move her car.

After that, I would often ask her sister how Arcira was doing, and did she say anything about me yet? Selene would always say yes, she told me to tell you "Hi". I found out later that Arcira never said that, it was Selene trying to get Arcira the hook up.

Soon, we went out on a date. She lived in Inglewood, and I lived in Whittier which is about 25 miles away. I would pick her up at her house, drive her back to my neighborhood for the date. At the end of the date I would drive her back to Inglewood, and then I would have to drive myself back to Whittier. That means, I drove about 100 miles every time we went out on a date. "If that ain't love I don't know what is?"

Time passed, and one day she had to go back to El Salvador for a visit. Those were some of the loneliest days of my life. When she came back, I could hardly wait, and I asked her to marry me. Let me tell you this, here we are, a black man, and a El Salvadorian woman, neither can hardly speak the other ones language, but ***"What God has joined together, let no man put asunder"***. This was indeed a match made in heaven.

Now back to 1993. We are married, and we have two boys, and somehow it felt so special. After several years of trying to find a church to attend, for some reason, we just couldn't find the right church to fit both of our cultures.

As I mentioned before, we were living in Federal Way, Washington, and one day I was shopping at the local Safeway store, and I saw a flyer on the community bulletin board. The flyer said someone was having a Bible study, the only other thing I could really understand was the phone number, because the flyer was done in Spanish. When I came out of the store, my hands were full, so I told Arcira to write down this number, and she did. We went home, and called the number on the flyer, and eventually decided to attend the next Bible study.

Fast forward a couple of months or so, and someone told us that we were the only ones to respond to that flyer I saw in Safeway. That tells me, that God was at work once again. No one else responded to that flyer, but us. There are lots of people going to that same Safeway, and only we responded. That's how God works, he works at the right time, in the right place, for the right purpose.

As we became more, and more familiar with the people at the bible study, we decided to join the church they were attending, and we knew that we had found a church that God had led us to. That church was started with less than 100 people, and today there is about 1500 members, and we have been there for over 20 years. ***"God is great and greatly to be praised."***

Chapter 2 – The Light Goes Out

Little did I know that in February of 2013 my life would be changed in such a dramatic way that I could not even imagine. I remember that day was a good day, I woke up just like every other day. When I think about it, just waking up was one of the things that I took for granted, just like most people do. I encourage you to give thanks to the one who allowed you to have another day of life. He continues to make miracles even if we don't see them or acknowledge them. God, and his grace is too precious to just throw it away. It is even too precious to throw away on petty anger. For one reason or

another we spend more time, and energy not speaking to family members, and friends then we ought to. We can do so much more if we keep our focus on God.

Each morning my wife would make breakfast for us, and I would take the boys to school. I remember how they would be so sleepy, and it was cold in the morning, the temperature was maybe about 35 degrees. As we drove on our way, I would let the window down, and man you can imagine what their face look like when the cold wind came in. Then I would sing to them, hurting their ears with the sounds I made. That was so much fun to see the expression on their faces. Well, maybe that was not such a good thing I did in the name of fun. When I look back at that day I'm sure it was not fun to them. When I dropped them off at school that day, little did I know that it would be the second to the last time I would see their faces, and expressions.

From there I went on my way to work. I talked to so many people that day. You see, I was an insurance salesman. Ironically I was talking to people about insurance, trying to help them be prepared for things that happen in life. As I was driving around going from place to place, there were people who requested quotes for insurance, and I told them I would get back to them the next day. So I headed to my office, and made some phone calls, ran some quotes. preparing to see them the next day. My day was winding down, and as I was getting ready to leave, I said those infamous words to some of my co-workers **"I'LL SEE YOU TOMORROW"**. Once again how strange that I would say that, not realizing what I was saying, in that I was taking God for granted. So I gathered up my belongings, got in my car, and begin to drive home to see my family. As I was driving looking at the lights change, the people walking in the streets, people waiting for buses, thinking that before I go home, I should stop, and get me a burger and fries, but I didn't, because I thought maybe another time, so I continued on home. When I got there it was so nice to be home, to begin to relax and watch a little football recap on TV. But then I always thought about the importance of family and how our time was spent. We had dinner together, we would ask, **how was everyone's day?** Some of the

stories were really funny, we talked about a lot of things. Once again not knowing what tomorrow was going to bring.

Later on as the night progressed my wife and I were preparing for bed and I told her there were a couple of things I needed to get ready for the next day. So I went to my office, and got busy. I took a little longer than I anticipated, once again not knowing what was in store for me the next day.

If I knew what tomorrow was going to bring, I would have taken a mental picture of my wife, a mental picture of what she look like, how beautiful her hair is, what beautiful brown eyes she has, tracing my hands around her face to remember the contours of her face, her nose and how she has this little dip in her chin and how soft and lovely her face felt to my touch. These were the things I thought about and that I would always see them. Once again, not knowing what was to come. That night as usual, we said our prayer together. As I relaxed and prepared to go to sleep, I reflected on the day and I thanked God for HIS grace for the day he allowed me to see, for it was truly the last time to close my eyes and see again. During that night he allowed me such a peaceful sleep, I slept like a baby. Before drifting off to sleep, I remember saying, *"Lord, help me to be prepared for the day you have in stored for me and my family"*.

It was the next morning now and I woke up to a pain in my eyes that I had never experienced before in my life. My head felt like it was going to explode. my body was shaking so hard, I was cold and sweaty all at the same time. My wife was next to me, holding me, I was screaming out because the pain was so great. I could not take the pain. Then I realized my condition and I said to her, *"I don't want to scare you, but I can't see"*. I told her to take me to the hospital. When we arrived in emergency, for some reason, my body was so tired as if I had not slept at all, I could barely walk. They had to put me in a wheel chair to take me in. The pain just would not stop. and I still could not

see. They put me into one of the emergency beds doctors came in and examined me, they ran several test but still could not figure out what was going on.

Eventually they gave me some medicines to help relieve some of the pain. Then they told my wife that I would have to go to another hospital that specializes in eye care. When we got there, it was a long wait before they could see me. When I was finally seen, they checked my eyes and determined that my eye pressure was really high. The normal pressure for eyes is 0 to 10 when they checked mines my eyes, the pressure was close to 70. They tried many different procedures in a attempt to get the pressure down. They finally explained what they needed to do. I was told they would have to insert a needle into my eye. The doctor explained the procedure, he said", the good news that you won't have to be put to sleep". I was saying to myself, **"WHY NOT"**. He continued to explain, "we will numb your eye with a gel, then we will commence with a series of poking your eye with tiny needles to determine if it is numb. Once my eye was numb, the doctor proceeded to take this seemingly large needle that looked to me like the size of a pencil and insert it slowly into my eye. Needless to say, I still felt that needle going into my eye and naturally, I tensed up as it was breaking the skin.

Amazingly, as I was going through the most traumatic and painful experience of my life, I still felt blessed, because, while all this was going on, my wife was right there by my side watching what was being done. They also found blood in my eyes and said will we'll wait to see if it will go away on its own, if not we may have to do surgery. I don't know about you, but me and surgery were not the best of friends. So I was sent home and given a time to come back to be re-examined.

We began to have appointment after appointment to see what could be done to save my eyesight. Every time we had appointments, we were in prayer asking God for a miracle. During this time we as a family were on an emotional rollercoaster. I can't even begin to imagine the suffering my family

was going through. I think about my wife, who was blaming herself, she told me **"I should have been taking better care of you"**.

Also during this time, my oldest son, EJ, who was in college, came to my wife and I to tell us that he was going to drop out of college because he was the oldest and felt like he needed to earn money to take care of us now. Wow! What a sacrifice my son was willing to endure for us. My wife and I began to pray and encouraged him to stay in college and finish what he has started.

Then there was my youngest son, Justin, he was also emotionally effected. He was praying and asking God for help, but felt he could not get a response from God. Also I know he was watching his father to see how I would respond to this trial.

As time progressed on, there were so many thoughts going on in my mind. One day I told the doctor that I was still having pain in one of my eyes. The doctor said. **"Well, if you continue to have this pain, we will have to take your eye out.** What? Wait a minute. That was a bombshell! Can you imagine what state of mind I was in, I've already lost my eyesight, now they are talking about actually losing the eye itself. Where can I find peace that can give me understanding during this time of such an emotional and physical trial? I began to ask God for strength and wisdom. It's not easy hearing that your sight is gone.

There was one time my wife and son had taken me to the doctor and as he was checking my eyes he said, *"Can you tell me when I flash this light in your eye is it on or off?"*

I responded to the light, but he was still determined that I could not see. So I asked him, *"If I can't see, how come I can see what you are wearing"*, he then ask me, *"What color is my tie?"* I told him it was blue. He was surprised, and said, *"What color is my medical jacket"*, I told him it was white, and I could see my son and my wife pointing up to God in praise, but all the doctor could say was *"Humm"*.

I know now that it was God letting me know it will be alright and it was His way of saying, *"No matter what they say, I am the doctor who heals not him"*. The doctor proceeded to tell me that there is no chance of me seeing again. My mind begin to race a 100 miles a minute. I took a deep breath and began to pray. I said *"Lord I know that with you all things are possible, I put my trust and my faith in you"*.

There were many days that I would go into my office and face my computer, knowing that I could not see. But I do know what I can do, and that is to pour out my heart and soul in pray, crying out wanting to connect with God. I said, *"I want to know what you want from me?"* Every day I would wake up early in the morning to listen for His voice and enter into his presence through praise and worship, preparing for my conversation with God. Listening to his word, renewing my mind, knowing that through all this time, he is the one who is giving me strength. He gave me the joy and the peace to continue to fight. He helped deal with the new challenges in my life and in the lives of my family. I'm truly learning what the Apostle Paul meant when he said, *"I can do all things through Christ which strengthens me."*

There were times when we would sit down to eat and for some reason, I would just begin to cry. My family would just be quiet and not say a word. They would simply get up from the table, come over to me and put their arms around me and gently say, ***"It's going to be alright."*** They helped me know that we are in this together. Thanks to my family, I was able to keep it together. This was one of the things that God did for all of us, he brought us closer together. I guess you can say he made us realize as a family, that he is first in our lives.

In our household, I was the bread winner for our family. But now, I began to think, what about my wife, what is she going to do and my boys, what about them. Statistics show that so many couples end up divorcing because they could not handle life's pitfalls. I thought about how much you must

trust in God's timing. I realized that my whole family had to deal with what was happening to me. But there was one thing I was sure of, and that was that we all were trying to trust in the one who has control over everything.

During this time many of the brothers and sisters from our church came to our house to visit, our house was often packed with people who loved and cared about us. They were also real prayer warriors who interceded on our behalf.

We were faced with the possibility of losing our home and not having enough food in the house, because there would be no income coming in. We didn't know what to do. One day my wife and I were praying, asking God for direction, and lo, he was with us, and behold there he was continually with us. We didn't know where to go or who could help us. The doctors didn't offer any ideas and so once again, we cried out to God to show us the way.

One day we were directed to a sister in our church, she had recently started working for the state of Washington as an interpreter for the blind. She eventually connected us with the Washington State Department for the Blind. Once we started interacting with them, we never saw her again. I say this to let you know, that God can use anyone at anytime, anywhere, if we choose to make ourselves available to his will.

When we step out on faith and begin to declare his will for our lives, he shows up and he shows up always on time.

Then reality comes and slap me hard in the face, yes I am human, but the God the I serve is the true doctor who can heal. But for some reason, when they issued me a cane for the blind, here I was a grown man, crying, because reality was setting in. I now realized this is real. And one more time, I asked the master for renewed strength, to help me through this. As I finished my session with the doctors, I don't know why but they always would ask me, was I depressed, but guess what my answer was, I said **NO!!!!** Then they would ask me why not. I responded, *"because I have a God who will never ever leave me and is with me through this trial".* Here's a strange note, after I was connected with the Department of the Blind, that sister from our church stop working for them and I never saw her again, not even in church. Now I don't know about you, but I just chalked that up to another sign *"that I am not alone".*

Then I had the task of telling my sibling that I was blind and that it was probably permanent. They said things like *"What do you mean you won't be able to see again".* Some were just silent and couldn't say much, and then came the tears and crying out, *"Oh my God".* But as for me, I remained encouraged, because of what God had in store for me. After the shock on the news of my blindness, each of my siblings in California, told me that they were amazed at how positive I was in the midst of this situation. They told me that I was an inspiration to them. But I knew that it was only by his grace that I am able to speak to him. This path that I am on now, I have never traveled this way before, but I do know that he is the answer to all my problems and prayers and that he is in control.

There were times when I thought things were getting better and I was in a place of progress. Here I am in a battle dealing with losing my eyesight, and lo and behold another trial comes. Being blind there are so many things that limits your ability to sense things, I don't know when or how, but one day I discovered a cut on my foot that had apparently been there for some time. But my most favorite nurse in the whole world, which is my wife came to my rescue. My foot was bleeding and as she was cleaning the blood away, she saw there was a cut beneath the blood. She would always check my feet from time to time because years earlier, I was diagnosed with type 2 diabetes. Diabetes can cause poor circulation in your legs and feet. Over the years I developed poor blood circulation in my feet, and I had little to no feeling in my feet. As a precautionary measure my feet had to be examined from time to time. We continued monitoring the cut for a while and it was not healing. In addition to the cut, my foot began to swell and the cut was getting bigger. Because of the swelling, It became harder

for me to put my shoes on. We decided to make another appointment with my doctor for further examination and after several more appointments and no improvement, she referred me to what they call the **Wound Care Center.** I said to myself, *"Here we go again".* So I did what I always do in times of stress, I begin to pray. I said to God, ***"Once again my trust is in you and through this trial may your name be glorified. Use me Lord that through me, may people will be lifted up".*** I guess you can say, it was me asking God to reveal his purpose for me.

At this point, I remember hearing how people deal with traumas and the difficult decisions we had to make. How many times when we make a decision did it work out? For the majority of us it turned out bad, because in our thought process our mind says, ***"I've just got to have it".*** I remember a customer came into the store where I was working one day and bought a big screen TV without consulting with his wife. As you can imagine, it caused that relationship a big problem. I said that, to say this, in all our decision making, we should seek God for wisdom first.

OK, Where was I? oh yeah, I was about to tell you about the **Wound Care Center.** They specialize in unusual wounds that have trouble healing. When they removed the wrapping there was this really bad odor. I knew this could not be a good sign, and the next thing I knew, they were sticking a needle in the wound and I didn't feel anything. They examined the wound inside and out, they even took measurements of the wound. They cleaned the wound and cut away some of the dead skin surrounding it to control the odor. Then they put on a new bandage and sent me home. After that, I visited the **Care Center** once a week for about 3 or 4 weeks. The wound still would not close, so they called in another specialist to help determine what was the next step should be. The decision was to take x-rays and then an MRI to see more around the cut. They discovered from the xray and the MRI that I had a bone infection.

When the doctors told me this, they gave me two options. One was to have surgery, saying they could go in and scrape the bone to see if they could remove the infection. The second option was to have me see another specialist specializing in **infection and disease** to figure out what the next step should be.

It has now been over two months since seeing the **infection and disease specialist.** They took a culture from the infected bone to see what was going on. After their examination they informed me that they wanted to try a stronger antibiotic for six weeks and it had to be administered intravenously. That meant that Ihad to a pick line inserted so I could receive the antibiotics everyday for the next six weeks.

During this time, the staff got to know me pretty well, because I went there always wanting to trust in the one that gives me life everyday and the people who were around me felt the love of God in my heart. When the staff saw me coming, they would say *"here comes trouble"* but it was meant in a good way. When things got worse, I would always remember what it says in Jeremiah 29 verses 11-13, ***"For I know the plans I have for you, declares the Lord, plans to prosper you and not to harm you, plans to give you hope and a future. 12 Then you will call on me and come and pray to me, and I will listen to you. 13 You will seek me and find me when you seek me with all your heart".***

Every day we all have trials, but it will also depend on us and where we are with God. We must renew our mind with the word of God everyday. (Romans 12:2)

When I went to church I told them what the doctor had said. They came and surrounded me and my wife and begin to pray. No one knows how hard it is until you have been there for yourself.

Chapter 3 - Which way to go?

There has been, there is and there will always be challenges in our lives. Our success in navigating the rough seas of turmoil that will rage in our lives depends on how we approach them. Sometimes we have a tendency to make them too small or too big.

I remember going through that turmoil when I lost my sight. My challenge was real to me, because I was living it. When I lost my sight I had to start over again, doing things like a baby who is learning how to take their first steps. If I wanted to go somewhere I could not do it. I had to adjust to the need to rely on someone to help me in things I was so adapt at doing myself. I had to figure out a way how to rise above my circumstances. I really had to come to grips with my new reality. My house was no longer a place of comfort for me but was a maze to be navigated through. The walls of my house and me became good friends.

Man, there were so many trials that came my way, it seemed as if they would never stop. My mornings became a time that I came closer to God. I would awaken early in the morning, go into a place created just for times like this, a place behind closed doors, not to hide from God, but a place that I would not be disturbed and have some "me time" with God. It started with wanting to have an intimate relationship with God. I would start just being silent asking God to come and be with me just for a little while. I was seeking his will in this time of my confusion. I would listen to songs of worship and praise, to help me enter into his presence. *I believe sometimes we have to stop and listen to what he is trying to tell us.*

My emotions were so high, I would be singing and praising him, crying out to him, not to say *"Why did you let this happen to me?"*, but to say *"Lord let your will be done in my life, because I know you have total control over my life, bring peace to my heart so that I will declare your glory."* There I was singing loud, praying loud, confessing loud, I knew that my family would be hearing me, but that was not important at the time. But, what was important was that moment. I also knew that whatever Ke was doing, He was doing it for my family. I knew that in my devotion to him, he would hear my cry.

There were times at church doing worship, God would break me down so strongly, that I would be a so into Him, and not worrying about what people would say, do, or think. I gave it all that was in me to him. I learned that if we make ourselves available to him doing our times of worship, He will do great things in our lives. Have you ever let go and just got into God and be touched by His great love? Those are the times when you really feel His presence.

I remember another time during the changes in my life when once again, while I was worshipping God, His spirit came pouring out over me. I didn't want to stop worshipping him, because I was focused on what He had already done for me. So with tears running down my face, and regardless of where I was, I asked my son to take me to the car, so I could continue being in His presence. This was when the main service was still going on. By the time I was done giving God all that is due Him the service was over. That's what I mean, **"When you are focused on him and not distracted, he can do powerful things!!!!" I can do all things threw Christ which strengthens me"** (Philippians 4:13). So I continue to hold on.

There will come times in our lives when it seems like it over and we want to give up, but it is really not over until the Master says it's over. We never knew how to fight a battle, but the word of God teaches us how to fight. I had to make some decisions, one of which was, **"How do I get training to survive in my new found condition?"** I could go to a training facility to help me adapt to these new challenges, learning how to care for myself , but I would have to live there for six months. Also, I would have to live with a roommate, someone I did not know. I had roommates when I was in college when I could see and that was not a good experience and this was something that just did not feel right. I already was nervous about what was happening in my life and now another curve ball was thrown at me.

If I decided to go to this training facility, I would have classes like computer training, Braille, cooking and mobility training. Mobility training is where they would teach me the rules of the road, how to use my cane properly and how to cross the street. I don't know how you would feel, if you were in my condition, but. it scared me that cars would be driving by and I couldn't see them. They also would teach me every day living skills like cooking. all these things would equip me for my future.

I thought about having long days of classes, then returning to my dorm room with nothing to do. But for me, there would always be something missing, my family. Family to me is very important, family is our support system. I felt that six to nine months away from them would seem like a lifetime. So after some time discussing this with my family we decided to look for other options. By the grace of God, we found another way. I could have someone come to my home and train me there. We prayed that God would open another door, because He was in control, and we as a family trusted in Him. We ask for wisdom in making the right decision. Wow, could it be that simple to just ask him for what you need, and declare in his name, ***"Not my will but yours will be done"***.

OK, back to my story. After we found another way to get the training I needed, we were excited that there would be someone to come to my home to teach me daily living skills. It was just as it sounds, they helped me get familiar with my surrounding. We had to put dots on things, to help me find the right buttons. Organizing things in the kitchen to help me find them again. Once that was done, I thought to myself, **"Here I am in the dark, not seeing anything, but knowing that God is with me Is so amazing"**.

I had to learn how to use a knife and not cut my finger off while learning, because, watch this, ***the person that was training me was also blind.*** what a pair! Only God can make a positive out of **"the blind**

leading the blind". Of course there were some mistakes and mishaps, but once I was familiar with the surrounding in the kitchen, I would say to myself, **"Look at what God is doing, I am in the dark, cutting fruit and vegetables and trying not to burn myself"**. Soon I was able to prepare a meal. One of the first meals that I made was a quiche. The instructor and I would pick a meal that I would prepare for her next visit. As time progressed, I learned how to prepare other meals. Eventually I was able to cook for the entire family. Needless to say, at times it was frustrating and challenging, and sometimes, yes, I would fail. However, in my mind, there would always be another day to succeed. This went on for almost a year and half.

Mobility Training

And once again, I had to rise up to the challenge of mobility training which taught me how to get around on the streets, it teaches you how to integrate yourself outside of the house. We began with training on residential streets. Out here on the streets, my nerves were coming and doubts were coming, **but because I have an awesome God,** I said, **"Let's get it on"**. We started with going around the block. I had to know my directions north, south, east and west, the things I never gave a thought to when I could see. But now I am walking as a blind person. Just like a baby, I am learning how to walk all over again. I was learning my directions, to know which way I was going and remembering how to get to different places on the street. When I can feel the sun on my face I know that I am facing east, that means west is behind me, south is to my right, and to my left is north. A lot of times in life when we can not understand basic direction, like what God says in His Word, how can we know which way God wants us to go.

One day my instructor gave me an address to locate by myself. When I told my wife about the assignment, she became very nervous, and worried. I proceeded on my assignment and I did good, finding the place for my assignment, but on the way back, I got confused and ended up in the middle of the street. "Good thing no cars came!" I realized standing there in the middle of the street, it was a lot like us in search of which way to go. And sometimes we will end up in the wrong place, but because of our faith in God, we have to know that God is in control. When you think about, God gives us protection and wisdom in making our decisions on which way to go.

After several sessions with my instructor, I was given the task of how to cross the street. Have you ever thought about crossing the street with your eyes closed? I know I have never given it a thought. So first I began by listening to the traffic for cars, to hear when it was safe to cross. I had to listen not only for the sound of the car but I had to also listen for the sound of the tires on the road. Needless to say, I don't like hybrid cars, because their engines are so quiet, I can't hear them at all, I only had about six second to get to the other side. Well, on my first attempt, I didn't make it to the other side, instead, I ended up walking diagonally toward the wrong corner.

Crossing commercial streets are a little more difficult, and stressful. One day I was with my instructor, and the plan was to cross the boulevard, While we were waiting for the light to change, a brother from my church saw me as he was driving by, and turned around and parked. He came over to me, on the corner, and asked if I was OK, and if I was here by myself. He also asked, if I knew this lady, who was standing on the corner next to me? I said, "Yes, she's with me, she's my instructor". This showed me that one of the ways God protects us is that he uses people in our lives to check on us to see if we are ok. So I want you to know that you are not alone.

Decisions are made every day of our lives. What to eat, what to do and how to do it. Statistics show that the high level of divorce is because of the amount of stress in the marriage. I thought it was hard already being a couple with just the basics of life, but now I know I was totally wrong.

I hear sad stories of marriages ending because one gets tired of the other. For example in a marriage one person loses the use of a body part and the other one cannot handle the stress of taking care of the the other one so they end up divorced.

What is it, when you make a decision after you have found someone who you care for so much, that you decide to start your life together. What kind of thought process was there to determine that final outcome? Was it because he thought she was hot? Or, was it because she thought this was the best she could do? Or, was it because she thought she may never get this chance again? Once again, we come to a point of a decision. I think when people are getting to know each other, when the man comes from a different background than the woman, it is two different people trying to mesh their lives together. And what happens when a child grows up with a father who is a workaholic, who has determined that the best way he can take care of his family is to work a lot of hours, or even take on a second job? Each decision we make in life can take us down a certain path. For example, someone says, ***"I am waiting on God to send me someone".*** Have you ever thought that, while you are waiting on God, his response is, I have already sent you someone, you just didn't see him or her, or perhaps we say to God, ***"Please provide me with a house"*** but God said, ***"I gave you an apartment and you can't even keep it clean"***. A lot of us want things just put in our laps, just so we could say it was God who did it. It took a decision that would choose their path in a way that they could not even imagine. The day that we make a decision, we don't know the outcome. As I reflect on my decisions, each one of them changed my path. Little did I know, God shows us that whatever we need, we have to work for it. Remember when Moses chose one representative from each of the twelve tribes of Israel to spy out the land of promise? Ten came back with negative reports, but Joshua and Caleb came back and

told Moses that we can take the land God has promised us. (Exodus 1 & 2) Or remember when Job was tested and loss everything he had including his children and his health. After all of his suffering, he became closer to God and in the end, he was blessed because God restored all of his riches including his children.

I sometimes wonder in my condition, how long will I suffer, but I know that every moment of every day, I am in a battle. Once again, I must make a decision. When we look at Gods plan for our lives, he gave us the choice to choose Him, because He knows that our choices can lead us down a different path.

I look at Adam and Eve and how God gave them specific instructions on what to do and how to do it. He also gave them instructions on what not to do. God's will is for us to make decisions with the understanding that what we do will change the direction of our path. It's kind of like, when you are driving a car and you have to make a decision on which way to go, how many times did you make a wrong turn and you ended up getting lost? If you had made the right choice, you would not have gotten lost, I know when Adam and Eve made their decision, it affected their lives forever.

The bible has many examples of decisions making that changed paths. One was when Moses's mother hid him from pharaoh's men who were killing all the young Hebrew boys. It was a decision that was hard to make, but she knew that in the long run, it would change the path of Moses.

What happens when a tragedy come in your life and you ask the question, ***"Why did this happen to me?"*** You get angry and frustrated, you get sad or depressed. When you should be saying, ***"I don't understand, but whatever it is, I know God is with me".*** How many times in the bible did you see so many tragedies? What about the story of Joseph who was thrown into a pit and then sold into slavery by his own brothers, but was deliver by God. You may not know what his plan is for your life, but I

can tell you this, **HE IS IN CONTROL**. We just need to have faith, even if it is as small as a grain of mustard seed.

God has given us a mind to think with, but instead of thinking of our blessings, we tend to think of our bad experiences. Our mind should be focused on God and His goodness, not about the bad things, like **"you are no good"** or **"you're not smart enough to handle that"**, and then you get depressed and sad and feel like there is no way out. You are walking down a dark road and you can't see the light at the end of that road. You don't know which way to go. I want you to know, the world has nothing to offer. I feel for the people who don't know God and don't know which way to go. They seek their reality in drugs, alcohol and abuse. The devil is always whispering in their ears. Listen to the story of Sodom and Gomorra when Lot's wife turned around, not able to let go of the place where she lived, where everyone was sinning. One thing I know, God gives us the ability to choose.

If you read the bible, He gives so many stories where decisions were made that changed their path. I know it's hard, but I know that there is hope in the God who created us. It is in his will that we examine the world, knowing that the world brings distractions to cloud our minds, so that we are not able to think clearly. My dear friends, it is a **"smoke screen"** that tells us, that if we had all the money the world has to offer, we would be in good shape. But I want you to know that if we live for God, he tells us that's not true. The devil says, **"Take those drugs so you can forget about all the great things God has in store for us"**. It is said that when on drugs, something is taken from us, drugs can be a devices the devil uses to trick us. If you think about it, if your brain is clear, you think differently. Obedience means doing the right thing, excepting what God wants for our lives, and to recognize that He is in control.

I don't know about you, but I can admit that some of the decisions that I made, were not the best. How many times do we make decisions without looking at all aspects of that situation. For instance, what would you do when you had to cross the street with your eyes closed, or what decision will you make when the time come? I think you have three choices; 1. Do nothing, 2. Procrastinate and 3. Use your God given ability to make a choice, after careful consideration and prayer. Do not make a snap decision. The goal is to have that intimate relationship with God. Also remember that God plans for you still continues to be molded and shaped regardless of the situation. Hold on to His hand and let Him do what He does best, love you unconditionally. No matter what comes, God says, ***"Be still and know that I am God."***

Chapter 4 - Changing Direction

When all this started, I did not realize that I could get lost in my own house. There were times when I would be restless and couldn't sleep, I would get out of bed and try to find my way through the house, like I knew where I was going! After a little while, my wife would realize that I wasn't in bed with her, and she would come looking for me. When she found me, I was standing in a corner, confused, because I didn't know where I was. I didn't know what to do or where to go. There I was in the corner, it's ironic that being in this corner was like being lost, in real life, and not knowing which way to go. With my new situation of blindness, I can identify with being lost. But if we can keep our minds on God we can know that we will understand it all later. Have you ever been in a situation that you felt that you were lost?

Do you remember when you went for a ride with your mom or your dad, and you knew you were leaving from your house, and you knew you were going somewhere? When you got to the destination you realized where you were, but what about all the stuff in between. Like which direction to go north, east, south or west. How did you get to your destinations? That's the same way life is, when something tragic happens. We know what "A" is and we know what "B" is, but what happened to all the stuff in between? When you look at my life, it has a beginning, a middle, but the end is still being written.

There was a story I heard about a young lady who lost her sight and did not want to do anything. She just stayed in her room, only came out to use the bathroom. Then she would go back into her room. She simply did not want to do anything, just be by herself. This young lady was like that for about five years, until one day she realized that there has to be something more. Well, that's what I believe also, I knew there had to be something more. Just because I lost my sight. I often found myself contemplating about how I was going to take care of my family.. Being blind, there definitely are challenges such as, trying to figure out what can I do to get my life situated. It was hard grasping on to how my life had evolved. Once again I was looking to change the direction of my life, trying to find out what is it that God has in store for me. The truth is, God tells me that, ***"he knows the plans that he has made for me"***. I'm learning that during these times, our times of struggle, God always takes care of us.

One day my wife came home and found a foreclosure notice on the door, she took the paper held it up to the sky and said, ***"I rebuke you Satan, in the name of Jesus"***. When I got home, she told me what she did. At first, I didn't get it, but what my wife did was express a declaration of Faith. Satan likes to throw arrows at us, but we can dodge and defer those arrows that come our way with this experience that we have with God. After further investigation, come to find out that there was a glitch in the mortgage company's computer system that caused them to mistakenly send out a foreclosure notice. But we had faith that God was protecting us, and He continues to do so. Know that during difficult times in our lives, He will show us the way. If we trust in Him and understand His truth, God will always be there for us.

How many times has it happen to you when you have been approached by some difficulty and you say, I have a problem. How did you deal with it? What were your resources? A lot of times we think we can do things on our own strength, but the thing is, we need to include God. A lot of times He is the extra push we need, because He is our real source of strength. We need to understand His truth and His plans for us. He didn't create us to make us suffer, He created us because of His love. God tells us in His Word, **just trust me and I will do things that you can't even imagine.**

So what happened? Let me take you down a road that shows you how God's truth can help you accomplish so many things. Remembering God's truth for example, Jesus says, ***"I am come that they might have life, and that you might have it more abundantly".*** That's the truth, because every day that we wake up, we have life. When we have life, we have the opportunity to be thankful that He's allowed us to live. Every opportunity that you have in life, God says, ***"There's something more for you"*** when you think that there's not enough. There's always more, because He gave you life. But, for some reason we take God for granted. Especially the little things, like the ability to walk, to talk, to see, and to hear. We sometimes take our spouses for granted by thinking they will always be there, doing whatever they do to make the family run smoothly. Children take their parents for granted by always thinking that they will do or give them anything they want. The parents may take for granted their children by not spending enough quality time with them before they are all grown up. Instead of taking God for granted, we should thank Him for all He does for us. So the question is, **"What will you do with what God has done?"** You can overcome anything with the help of God. He says, ***"I am with you all the way, even till the end of time".***

Have you ever thought that God has abandoned you? Well, here's another truth. Here I am a blind person, trying to learn things like how to use a computer, how to cook and do different things. Before my blindness, I was a salesman, I sold insurance, I sold "life insurance", "automobile insurance" and "homeowners insurance". It was a very hard thing to do, but one thing I learned was that life was important to me, and it motivated me to help people understand the process of life, and the things that life is really all about. Knowing the necessities of life, and how to be thankful for what you have.

Once there was a couple that I spoke to about purchasing insurance from me. They already had homeowner's and automobile insurance, so I started speaking to them about life insurance. Explaining the pros and cons and benefits, but to make a long story short, I tried to convince her husband to purchase life insurance to protect his family. They did not give me their answer that day. A few days later his wife called me and asked if her husband had gotten the life insurance, I told her ***"No, he didn't get it".*** She told me that the reason she asked was because her husband was in a automobile accident and died. Sometimes we have to learn how to appreciate life to its fullest, making every day, every hour, every minute count. Feeling sorry for ourselves after a tragedy has occurred doesn't help, but giving thanks to God for everything He's done for us is what we should do.

It's a tremendous feeling when you can trust in God and believe in his plan for your life. Here's what happened to me. Being blind was very difficult, but in order to start my own insurance agency, I had to create a business plan, I had to go before sponsorship panel that would give me financial help to start my own business, as an independent Insurance Agent. Never did I think I could do it, but I was determined, and it was because of my faith in God. I knew He would give me wisdom and guidance, that He was in control and was always with me.

I want you to know that God has great plans for us, but we have to make ourselves available to His plans. His truth cannot be denied because of who He is. He's also the one that continues to spread His love among all of us.

You do know that it is because of God that we have life. But, are we being thankful for the life that we are given?

Think about it, every time we wake up we have life, regardless of the circumstances. We can choose to focus on our problems and situations or we can just be thankful for being alive and for the opportunities that life brings

We need to be thankful for that life, we wake up complaining about things, but we should be saying thank you for my life today, it's because of you that I live. Let me tell you something, it is because of his love that we have a life and with that life, we need to be thankful for all he has given us. He has made plans for us each step of the way regardless of our situations, problems, or any other concerns we may have. We should realize that we have life and all God is saying is, ***"What can you do to make a difference today".*** Remember each day that you have life, you have an opportunity to make a difference,

Let me use the LOVE to encourage you to see how much God cares about you

L stands for life – Jesus says, ***"...I am come that they might have life, and that they might have it more abundantly"..***

O is for obedience – to His word and His will for our life and knowing that His word is true, and that you have chosen to obey Him.

V is for victories - sometimes when we think about the victories that we don't have, we don't look at the small victories as a victory at all. For example, you might say, "hey, I just received one million dollars". Now that's a victory. But because that was such a large victory, we over look the smaller victories in our lives. Like hey, I'm still able to see, I'm still am able to talk, I'm still able to worship God. All of these are victories that God has given us as well. He wants us to be victorious in His name, therefore, we have to keep fighting, and don't give up, knowing the truth will set you free.

E is for everlasting - As you think about everlasting, God said I am with you all the way even to the end of time. Do you know what infinite means? It means He will never stop,. He will never end, and He will always love you, regardless of what is going on in your life.

We need to realize that our life is not ours, it belongs to God, and it's not our will, but His will be done. And when you understand that you have a purpose here on this earth, God will continue to show you the life and the way. The Bible says He is ***"The way, the life and the truth..."***

We must learn how to prepare ourselves for the great love He wants to give each and every one of us, every day and every step of the way. Now that's the truth, and the truth is that God loves you regardless.

CHAPTER 5 – LIVING THE DREAMS OF GOD –

What it boils down to is this, **"to have faith in God"**, no matter how small or how large your faith is, He has great things for you. Believe in the great plans for your life, that God has in store for you. Trust in the one that created you for his purpose. Be available to his will in your life, creating the connection that says Lord, I want to be close to you, take my hand, and lead. I am not saying that it's going to be easy to do it, but I am saying, it's going to be well worth it, to have peace in your life. Knowing that God has control over everything, you mind, heart, and soul give it all to him, so that he can begin to create those promises that he has for you.

Never could I have imagined not seeing my wife's beautiful eyes, and beautiful smile, when I said bad jokes. Never could I have imagined not seeing my sons faces, and how they react when I would tell a joke or when I would always beat them when we played video games. Never could I have imagined that I wouldn't see the face of my grandchildren growing up, but I do know one thing, I can see the promises in the dreams that God has in store for me. I have realized that we have to learn how to live in the dream, knowing that God is everything to us.

During this journey of change, I find that I have a close relationship with God. I think that in the special moments when you are trying to connect with God, you have to believe in what He has for you, and that He will help you through the difficult times. Sometime when we dream, we have a tendency to dream small. We must be able to dream big, because our God is a big God, and he gives us the knowledge to believe in ourselves.

There are times when our thoughts can be redirected, like when you have to go to the bathroom really bad, and then something distracts you, and now you don't have to go as badly as you thought. That's the time that God is showing us that we don't have to worry about some of the small thing in order to stay focused on the bigger dream.

I'm reminded of the bible story of Joseph who had dreams of his future, but he didn't understand it at the time. And his jealous brothers threw him into a pit, and then sold him into slavery. However, God never left Joseph, and continued to work in his life, even in captivity. The future is ours, if we choose to dream. When we look at the life of Joseph, we see that he didn't know what was going to happen to him in the future, but had unwavering faith in knowing, that God had a plan for his life, even though he was in captivity. And just like Joseph, God has a plan for our lives, every step of the way. We won't realize that he's taking us to certain places, until we get there. But we have to be willing to change directions, and go where he leads.

Whatever I went through in my past, I know now that I am in a better place. Because, as I think about it in my mind, and visualize what it looked like, I know that life is worth living in the dreams of God.

Maybe, I can't see physically but I can see spiritually. I think about the things that I could do when I could see. I realize now, that when I could see, what a blessing I had. I know a lot of times we often take those things for granted, not looking for the lessons that could be learned from our difficult situations. Became even more evident, a lot of times we get distracted with some of the things that we are entertained with. I know I lost my inspiration to be focused on God through the distractions of my circumstances, and situation, when I know that he has plans that are made just for me.

What about the times that we so easily forget about the things he's done for us because we are overwhelmed with all the distractions in our lives. am encouraged when I think about some of those dreams that were given by God to so many different people in the Bible. I'm not saying that before I

lost my sight, everything was a bed of roses, it wasn't. I am still in a transition mode, to adapt to change, and being challenged by the plan

God has for me. A lot of times we continue to fight the wrong battle, instead of giving it to God. Yes there are challenges, and yes there will be some good times, and some bad times, some ups, and some downs, but that's all part of life. Knowing that I don't have to face these challenges alone bring joy, and relief to me.

Throughout your whole life there's always been problems, throughout your whole life there has always been ups, and downs, But, do you know that even in the Bible, there were times that were difficult. There were times when Peter, walk with Jesus every day, but he also denied Jesus three times in one night, So I know that we will be in battles, but my thought is we have to learn how to deal with each time, and each problem as they come. The battles that I have had, and the problems that I have had to face, have all become a part of being blind, and trying to find, and make some sense of what's happening in my life. It took a lot, but I have resolved in my life, that I am a true child of God, and because I have life, I am able to focus not on the bad things, but the good things. I've decided to be focused on the life, and opportunity that I was given, no matter how big or how small the distractions are, I know that God will continue to work in my life.

I've decided to give my heart, my soul, and my mind to God, I know that because of him, I am valued, and I bring value to those around me. He has taught us how to be humble. He has taught us how to be grateful, and he has also taught us how to love one another. God has taught us that we are special in his eyes, regardless of the circumstances of all the things that have happened in our lives.

So the choice that comes down to you today, is, ***"What will you do in following Jesus"?*** I've spoken to many people who were going through some difficult times, and a lot of the questions they asked were, ***"If God loves me, why did he let this happen to me?" "If God love me, why do I feel so lonely?"*** Or ***"If God loves me, why do I have to have such a difficult life"?***

When things happen in our lives, we tend to only remember the bad things, but God remembers everything, God knows what you're going through, he feels what you're going through, but we say God doesn't love me. Every time something happens to you, as a tear drops, God knows your pain, and your suffering. But He says, **"All you have to do, is listen to me, and I will help you through it"**. We grow, and learn from the things that happened in the past, bad and good. When I'm going through those difficult times, I look for God's arms to be open wide to hold me tight, and to tell me that everything will be OK.

We have to learn how to trust in God, and figure out how much love God has for each, and every one of us,. Half the battle is knowing when to be encouraged to fight, because we know that it's possible through God. But we give up, we feel bad about ourselves, and begin to think, why me. All of that struggle does not mean you are defeated, but if you stand firm on the word of God, he will give you the victory. Do you know what I mean? Before Moses, and the children of Israel could enter into the Promised land God did not simply give it into their hands they have to fight for it. They had to go forward, and make sure that God's plan for them would be done.

There is a story about a man who died and went to heaven. An angel greeted him at the pearly gates, and took him on a tour of heaven's grandeur. Along the way, the man noticed an unusual building with no windows, and only one door. Asking to see it, the man was advised that he really would not want to see what was inside. But the man pleaded to see inside the building. Once inside, he saw rows, and rows of shelves from the floor to ceiling, all filled with beautifully decorated boxes.

Examining them further, he found a large group of many boxes that had his name written on the tags. The man asked, why are all these boxes here with my name on them? The angel replied, "Inside these boxes are the blessings God had given to you, that you didn't ask for or you never opened."

That doesn't mean that every time we ask for something, God's going to say yes. The way we look at it is, when we receive something, we immediately say, "God heard my prayer". Well, God hears every prayer, every time you get down on your knees, and pray. It may be a simple prayer or a long prayer or a short prayer, it doesn't matter, because he hears every prayer.

I had already lost a brother, and a sister, and in 2005, another one of my brothers passed away from a heart attack.

Three days later my mother passed away from a broken heart, because of the passing of her children before her. it's not up to us to question God, and say, *"God, why did you let this happen?"* Rather we should learn how to be humble enough to say, *"Lord let your will be done because you have control over everything thing that will happen in our lives".* I pray that all can reach this level of faith, because I've learned to let the will of God be done in my life. So when tragic things happen in your life, know that God is with you, know that God has control, and know that God still has a plan for you. No more pointing fingers at everyone, point to the father, who gave you life, and the reason you're still here today. Be strong, be encouraged to, *"fight the good fight of faith".* The Apostle Paul talks about standing up for the truth, the truth is, *"yes, tragic things do happen".* However, because of the promises of God, there is no reason to feel sorry for yourself. When difficult times come you can turn it around. I don't think I would have be able to learn how to work on a computer or work through mobility training or even learn how to find my way around or cook in the kitchen, if I didn't trust in God When this tragedy came into my life, I could have settled for doing nothing, I could have

stayed in my room, but I chose to invest in myself by investing in God. Instead of just sleeping my life away, I chose to step out on faith, and LIVE THE DREAMS OF GOD.

Chapter 6 – Believe

Here's what it boils down to, you have to believe in the God that created you, the God that has a purpose specifically for you. The decisions that you made changed the path of which you were traveling. The choices that you made may not have been the best choices, regardless of the circumstances or situations you were in or the problems you had. The bottom line is that you must believe in the one who created you. So what I'm saying is, always, before those decisions, and choices are made, consult in the highest level to change your direction. Always remember to include God in the decision process, pray to him to help you make the right decision.

God created you with a plan for your life. You may not know what it is, but in Gods time, it will be revealed to you. It's like climbing up a mountain trying to reach the top. The higher you climb the thinner the air gets and the harder it is. But once you reach the top, looking back down the mountain you know that God was with you every step of the way.

You are a child of God, believing and trusting that he knows your sorrows, your sadness, and your brokenness, but he wants to fix you. The love of the father will never end. Believe in who you are, believe that God is with you, believe that there is so much more in your life, believe in the power that God has put inside of you. It's like when you're being put in a corner, you have to fight, stand firm, and don't be afraid. But, regardless let God be with you every step of the way. Seek the connection with him to help you through it. Start your day with a positive word that you can focus on, so that you are appreciative for the life and the time that God has given you. Let your heart and mind believe in

the one who created you, because God wants to take you on a journey of love and peace. Your journey has just begun and it will never end until God says so. So take hold of his hand so you can be assured that you'll survive your journey. You'll grow more and more as long as your faith, your trust, and your love is in God. Just remember who you are, what you are, and why you are so beautifully and wonderfully made by the creator of the universe, our God.

It is not mistakes that limit us, it's fear. Every day you wake up, you have an opportunity to make a difference in your future, to believe it is tangible, and real, but you have to believe in you who the creator made. Great works awaits you when you understand that you must believe in God, and yourself. If you wake up in the morning and you look at yourself in the mirror, it is real, you see it, but it doesn't have to define you, because you're looking at the physical.

You need to begin to look inside of you. As long as you have a brain you can tell your brain anything you want to, but the catch is believing and looking inside yourself to discover all the many different things that God has placed inside of you. Many times we let the world dictate who we are. You know we see those commercials that shows a man being ripped with a tight stomach, a tight chest and big muscles. You'll see a woman who has a great figure. The world says you have to create who you are, but God gave you the ability to choose, and it's up to you to choose the correct way you look at yourself.

Why do we always look at the other person, and say *"That person looks better than me?"* When inside that person could be suffering, and having extreme difficulties, because they work so hard to keep that outward look.

I remember seeing a story where there was a girl that thought she was ugly, so she would stay in her room, and write little Post-it notes to herself, saying positive thoughts about who she was. Little did she know she was only looking on the outside, and felt she was inferior or could not live up to the outside.

Even when I could see, I was never concerned about the outside, and what I looked like, because I told myself on the inside, I'm happy, I'm satisfied with who I am, I am content with who God created in me. Friends, that is the strongest thing you can ever do, because you're not focusing on the outside or what society says you should be, but you're focusing on the inside, and what God has told you who you are. When you feel that you're not doing the best you can, think again, God gave us a brain to mentally interpret the things of this world.

Have you ever thought about how we have been given a life, but we continue to let the world around us control it, when the one that is in control, is God. If we just strive to please God, he will take care of everything else. Your thoughts, your habits, all these things can be changed. but once again it depends on you. You have to make the choice.

We can have positive thoughts, if we choose to, but every day we are bombarded with so many different negative things. If you believe within your heart, you will know who you are. You will know, you are the one that can make a difference in your life, and in the lives of others. The ability to have positive reinforcements in, and around you will help you connect to God. Starting the day with positive thoughts can affect the outcome of that day. Let's just say you select "thankful" as your word for the day, thankful for what you are, thankful for your family, thankful for what God has done for you, for that day. Just starting out with a positive word, like "thankful", thinking about how thankful

you are about what God has done for you that day. Every day start out with a positive thought, so you will be in control what happens that day. When thinking positive thoughts, it helps during the day, instead of always looking at the negative things, and making it bigger than it needs to be. Let the positive thoughts overcome those negative thoughts so that when you think about the one who created you, it's all good.

Nothing can take that away from you, because of the plan that He has for you. The negative things that are going on in your life are not as big as God. Train yourself, teach yourself, believe in yourself, because when you begin to believe in yourself, in bold confidence of who you are, and what you are, you will kmow your purpose is in life.

I remember back when I was playing sports, and people would tell me that I wouldn't make the team. Well once again, I made a choice not to believe in what they were telling me. I believed in who I was, and what I was capable of doing. That's the power of God saying to me ***"You can do anything you want to do, all you have to do is, just believe in me, and I'll believe in you. You are greater than you ever thought you could be".***

You know, I always felt that my relationship with my natural father wasn't the best, but it was a relationship. I know that sometimes when we look at our parents, and then we look at our children, we know that we could have better affected how they grew up. But guess what, doing this time of blindness, I discovered that there is my heavenly Father, who's always had in my life. A father that I can talk to, a father that continues to be with me regardless of anything that I may have done. You have the same father, and hope, so you should believe that He is willing to do anything for you, believing is one of the strongest things you could ever do. I don't know you, but I discovered that I

don't have to be a star to know who I am, I don't have to be famous to know who I am, because I know who I am. When you learn or when you begin to know who you are, things will begin to change for you. When you believe in what you are capable of doing, when you believe that even when life looks dark, you can overcome that darkness. It depends on you.

I know that we will have struggles in life, but it boils down to believing in who you are, and what you were created for. Most of all, I bet you can tell yourself over, and over again how many mistakes you've made, and how many things that have gone wrong in your life. Why did those things have to go wrong in your life? You have to learn how to accept the mistakes that you make. You must also know that there is something to learn from those mistakes, those decisions, and those thoughts, that were made in error. Remember, you can change the outcome of your life, it just depends on, if you can BELIEVE.

Chapter 7 – Feeling Good

When do you begin to **feel good** about who you are? When do you begin to recognize it's good to feel good about who you are? When you look back at your parents, and how you were raised, Is it what your parents did, and how they treated you? While growing up my parents were separated, so I spent half the time living with my dad, and half the time living with my mother. I think I turned out OK. But once again I believed in God, and I believed in myself, and who I was. It may take some time to get to that point, but you can do it. Yes, I know you may have had a single mother or a single father. And yes, I know your struggles are real because my struggles are real. I grew up living in Watts, a small community in South Central Los Angeles. Living in times that were difficult, but that did not define me, or who I am. By learning how to **feel good** about your progress, or the steps you've taken, define who ou will be.

I remember the times when I went to the beach, and contemplated life, and what it meant to me, where I was at the time, and even where I was going to be in the future. Times like these is when we should seek guidance from someone else, a special counselor, not being afraid of who you are, but being comfortable to talk to someone that is willing to listen. However, it's hard to find those that are really willing to listen. A lot of times we are not looking for answers, we are not looking for resolution, we're only looking for someone willing to listen. Who better that is willing to listen then God.

I know that there will be times in my life where I'm just not going to be **"feeling good"** about who I am. I also know that I can change how I feel about myself in my appearance, but how I feel about myself on the inside? There is a times when you may feel like you are not worth anything. Thoughts run through your mind, like, **"Why was I born?"** or **"What have I done?"** Sometimes we look to blame ourselves, when really the responsibilty is not ours. But there are those around you who blame you or use you as a scapegoat for their problems. Even some parents who cannot handle the responsibilities of parenthood, blame their children, and the children come away wondering **"What did I do for my parents not to want me?"**

The insecurities, and low self-esteem that we have, is because we haven't begun to discover who we are, what is our potential, or what are the possibilities in our lives. Do you think that when you were born, you were meant to be nothing , a nobody, an alcoholic or a drug addict?" Well I beg to differ, your birth was not an accident, it was a miracle. God continues to bless us, but we look at it, as if we are the problem, but we're not the problem. So when do you begin to **feel good** about who you are? Will you let others determine when you feel good? So you think you need other people in order for

you **feel good, well** I don't think so. If you believe in who you are, **feeling good** is a mental state of mind. Will you have trust in God? What will it take for you to **feel good** about yourself? Number one, recognize that you are a miracle, and a child of God.

Number two, don't let people stop you from believing in who you are. Number three, you are in control of your destiny. Number four, believe that God has plans for your life, and that he has promised to take care of you.

Now let's begin to change your mind, and the way you understand who you are, where you came from, and where you could go, knowing the possibilities are limitless, because of who you are. **Feeling good** about who you are makes a difference in every way of life. Such as going to work, going to school, going to play, or going to different places. It can make a difference! Let's say, when you go on an job interview, what did you have to do before that interview? Well, you had to prepare a resume, which means, you were able to write about yourself , tell others what you're capable of doing. Now you have to get ready for the interview. During the time you're preparing for the interview, you make sure you know where you going, because you want to be there on time. Now you are at the interview. You're sitting with the interviewer and they begin to inquire about who you are. Are you nervous or are you confident about who you are, and what you bring to the table? You have to talk to yourself, shake yourself, be alert so you will be ready to answer any question they may ask. The goal is, you have to be confident in who you are!

So every day that you get up, and get ready to go to work, is a matter of believing in who you are. Every day when you get up, and get ready to go to school, is a matter of believing in who you are, and not being influenced by outside sources. Such as your peers, your coworkers, even some family members, and even some leaders at church. Be confident, let people begin to see something special in

you, because you are created special. Let people see you in victory, over your struggles, and difficult times. God will continue to strengthen you, because you are heroes. Let people see you being a star, and you can say, **"I am who I am, because God created me that way"**. You may not be able to see where you're going, but you know which way to go to get there.

I remember when I was in training for the blind, I was staying at a hotel, and I had to call for a cab to take me to the training center. The cab came, and picked me up, as we're driving, the cab driver was trying to talk to me, and make me feel good, and comfortable. He asked me a question, and my response was, " I don't know". Or he'd ask, " **Have you seen this building or that building?"** I'm sitting there, and thinking to myself, **"Hey man, I'm blind, do you think I've seen that building?"** Whether we're blind, or whatever handicap it is, even being normal you are special. Please stop letting the world influence you! Rather, let us influence the world by showing the characteristics of having faith, hope, and trust in a God.

May the Lord continue to show us new, and different things every single day of our lives. It's time to start standing up and recognizing who you are, and feeling good about how wonderful the journey is that you're on, and that it is special, and unique to you alone.

Remember that your victories can always, and will always be from the God who loves you, for who you are. So start your new journey, let your mind be renewed, start to **feel good** about you! And don't forget this, **"All things are possible, when you trust in the God who created you."**

Thank you for joining me on my journey. A journey of FAMILY, experiencing the LIGHTS GOING OUT, being confused, and learning WHICH WAY TO GO, choosing to CHANGE DIRECTIONS in

order to LIVE IN THE DREAMS OF GOD, it was all possible because I had the courage TO BELIEVE, and while my journey is not ober, I am FEELING GOOD in who I am..

May God bless all who read this book, as you continue on "your journey of life" with the God of all creation, being guided by his spirit, and believing in his son.

24 Now unto him that is able to keep you from falling, and to present you faultless before the presence of his glory with exceeding joy, 25 To the only wise God our Saviour, be glory and majesty, dominion and power, both now and ever. Amen. (Jude 24-25)

Chapter 8 - Lord you complete me

Yes it's true that society is an indicator of our excess or success whether you are tall, short, fat, skinny, long haired or short haired. Or is it cool that I have the right color hair or wear the right dress to match with the right color purse and the right color shoes. For a man, to be able to wear the right shirt and the right shoes, is that cool? Or what does it mean to be hip. I am consumed with what people think about me or what they say about me. Society makes us feel guilty for wanting to be who we want to be, but if we don't look or dress or have a certain haircut, then we're not meeting the expectations of society. If I do drugs, am I cool? If I drink alcohol when I go out, am I cool?

Society tells us it's OK to expose little boys and girls to adult things Teenagers are in relationships when they haven't even learned what love is all about, and they're having sex at a young age. It's cool to society that unmarried adults are living together, to test whether their relationship will work or will not work.

Well, guess what, you'll never know until you do it the right way. However society wants us to believe we're already doing it the right way, but society is giving us false impressions.

If I have a nice-looking car, I'm cool, right? But that nice-looking car is putting me further into debt. If we look a certain way, if we drive certain cars, we can be acceptable in eyes of society.

Have you ever tried to put a round peg in a square hole? It doesn't fit. Society tries to mode us and shape into some all encompassing way that we should be, but it doesn't leave room for being who you really are. Before I lost my sight I used to enjoy going to the movies by myself. The maker of movies gives us a beginning, a middle, and an end. Have you ever seen one of those movies or TV shows where there is seemingly a perfect family, they are always doing well, there are no problems in their world. It's what I call, **"The Leave It To Beaver Syndrome.** There are always differences and difficulties in family life, now that's reality, while the movies wants us to believe that what we see on the screen is real. With relationships, like when a boy or a man meets a girl or a woman, society continues to tell us how that relationship should be formed or created and how it's supposed work.

For instance, when a girl and boy meet, they begin to date and get to know each other. Then they decide to live together because society says it's OK and then they decide to get married. But the reality of a true relationship is based on commitment to the unknown. The willingness to step out on faith.

We are always looking for something to help us identify and confirm our lives, society says if I drive or do something different and don't fit in to the bubble that's created by them, I'm an outcast. Society sets a high bar for us to reach before we can be considered hip and cool by societies idealism, that says, you must be this way in order to fit in.

Have you ever wondered where these standards come from or how we came to an existence that we can never meet its expectations? It is sad that young people today at the age of 12 or 13 are considering suicide, because of the unrealistic expectations, they are made to believe that they don't fit in with their peers. I never thought that kids would be thinking in that way.

There was a story of a 13 year old girl who was being bullied at school. She couldn't talk to her parents, she couldn't talk to her friends, she felt as if she couldn't talk to anyone So this precious little girl ended up committing suicide, simply because she was made to feel that she didn't fit in.

And what about other girls, they have a lot of pressure to look like society says they should look or boys growing up with the pressure that society says they need to be a certain way. That's society setting the standard. There is so much pressure for us not to be able to look like the person that God created in us. When Moses went out to see the burning bush, God told him to tell the people "I am that I am" We have to look at that as well, society says you need to be this way but you can them "I am who I am", and that's all right with me.

If we don't focus on what society says, and instead focus on who we are. We won't have to worry about being hip or cool. worrying about if I have too much hair or not enough hair or am I fat, am I skinny or am I different. How do you evaluate your level of esteem, are you at middle, low or do you have no esteem at all. If you have low esteem, it's only because you have not tapped into learning about who you are. Instead of trying to fit in to society, let's beginning to make society fit into who we are.

There are options and choices that we must make. The Bible teaches us who we are, what we are, and what we can be. Instead of chasing society, let's turn the tables and let society chase us, and not have society be our idols. But let God be the leader of our lives. Let's not forget who created us, he knew us before we were born. He is the one who gave you everything you have. Remember God is not concerned with how you look, you've already met his approval because you are his child.

While growing up, if you have a relationship with God, he teaches you that you are special to him. He shows you that he has a plan for you. He shows you that his promises are true, and that he will never break a promise to you. I remember when I was growing up, my parents split up and I live half the time with my mother and half the time with my father. While living with my mom, there were many difficult times. Some of them were violent because of the way society allowed us to live outside of common sense boundaries.

I remember when my older brother found out that when you turn 18, it was time for him to leave the home, because society says that's the way it was done. But sometimes society sends you in the wrong direction, because you haven't figured out who you are and how special you are. And there's always more to it than you think.

Have you ever thought about when something happens and you end up crying and thinking you're all alone? Well you were never all alone,

God sees every tear that fell from your eyes, and he has cried right along with you and for you. To think that you're alone is wrong, because when we were created, we are given the ability to learn and know who we are and who created us..

The decisions we make are what creates who we are. Even when you were a child growing up there were decisions that you made that changed the way you are today. Did you know that we were not

created to worry or to be in fear, but we were created to worship the God. We need to learn to trust and to have the hope of a life that when we have God on our side we have our own dance partner, we have our own party friend, in him. We have everything we need. We just need to learn how to be content within ourselves, regardless of what we look like on the outside. We must realize that we were created with a purpose, with promises that will be everlasting for each and every one of us. That you and I are wonderfully and marvelously made in his image. And that we may know that all the difficult times that we go through, that he is right there with us and it will be alright, because we were made and created by God. And I challenge you to look within yourself and know that you have the best of the best, because of who created you.

Therefore, I encourage you through my prayers that you will learn to love yourself as God loves you. After growing up and learning who you are and that because you trust and have faith in who you are, you can say. Lord, complete me, to be the best that you can be and because of you God, I know that I am never alone. Because of you Lord, and your love for me, I can now confess that you are sufficient for my life. Amen.

Chapter 9 - IN HIS PRESENCE

Where to begin? Let's look at some things that will help us to start seeking his presence. We have evaluated ourselves and our surroundings or situations and we realized how special God has made us and now we recognize who we are.

Have you ever asked yourself what is the difference between the words "want" and "desire". Well, I looked up the definition of the word "want", it means, "the lack of not having". For example, let's say you're hungry. You "want" to eat in order to facilitate that lack. Or if you're thirsty. You "want" to

drink something in order to quench that thirst. The definition goes on to say that "want" is an action word, that means if you "want" something, you have to put something into motion to achieve that "want".

I also looked at the word "desire". What is desire? Desire is "something you wish for or long for", in other words desire is something you hope for. Now I have a better understanding of Hebrews chapter 11 verse 1, where it says, "faith is of things hoped for and the evidence of things not yet seen." So desire to me says, If I desire to stand firm, I'm saying I have hope to stand firm because I have trust and faith in a God that's everything to me. That's why I have a "desire" to have that special place where I can have an intimate relationship with God. A place that gives me peace, a place where I can just be alone with my creator. A place where I can cry or scream and know that he's right there with me.

Desire is that desperation of wanting be in that intimate place with God so badly, but not knowing how to get. Wanting to have a place that gives me peace, and where I can be alone with God. I've learned that it starts with prayer.

How do I pray? Is it a long drawn out prayer? Is it a short prayer? You should remember God already knows what you need, so all you have to do is focus on him.

You first have to find that special place that gives you privacy, a place that is peaceful and quiet, where you and God can commune together. A place where you can set your mind and focused on him without any distractions, so that you can begin your intimate relationship with God,

Once you find your special place, go into that place, not wanting anything from God except a desire to be in his presence. Now you can begin to have that relationship with him that you've wanted for

such a long time. When you go into that special place, don't worry about outside distractions, don't worry about the things that you can't do anything about, just focus on him, worship him and let your heart be filled with his love. And if you want, let your tears run free, and let your voice screen out, then be still and let your voice be silent and most of all, let his spirit flow within you.

Imagine you are sitting by a running tiver. You're sitting there just asking to be in his presence, and God comes and sits right beside you. He begins to tell you about the love that he has for you, about how he is so excited for the things he has in store for you, and that he's so glad you are here with him. Those are the times that allow God the opportunity to listen to you, to cry with you, to hold you, and then peace comes, because he tell you "everything is gonna be all right".

Sometimes I think back when I first lost my sight, when I had to find that secret place and I thought "Lord there is no one like you". And from that thought I begin to realize how true that statement really was. How he has done what he has done in my life, how he continues to shape and create everything about me to be special.

Can you imagine walking hand in hand with Jesus as he continues to make you so happy to be in his presence? I think we all want to be happy, but the most important thing is we have to be happy in him. Not disappointed and frustrated in the affairs of this world, but just thankful he's there with us every step of the way.

Do you remember the times when you would cry and cry and cry when something really bad happened in your life? Well this is what you do, you pour out everything you have inside of you to him, everything in your mind, your heart, and your soul, just to be in his presence. You don't continue to let anything hold you back, regardless of the circumstances or whatever is going on in

your life. Just focus on him, tis is your way of saying I want to be with you not just right now but all the time. It makes a difference when you pray from your heart because with your heart you sing, **"Lord take my heart mode me and shape me, but know that my heart is tender enough so that you can hold it and caress it, so that I can begin to experience the type of love that you have for me".** This is what we do when we open our hearts to God.

There is nothing that he can't do, it's just that we limit him and ourselves because we don't let go of the things of the world. When we learn how to let go of ourselves, it starts a new beginning for us to feel our emotions running through us to know that God is with us. It's your spirit being inspired to keep him and focus on him every step of the way.

When you go into his presence, it is a time of thankfulness. When you think about being thankful for what he has done for you. It's because of him, you are who you are, but you have not learned how to let him in. That's why you look for that secret place, that place that you can call yours, that place where you and God can be alone, sharing that intimate time, praying to him to help you. Not to say I want this or that, but to say, **"Lord, I want to do your will, I want to have an intimate relationship with you".**

Don't be afraid to expose your heart to him, he already knows who you are. You have to acknowledge him and then be willing to let yourself be opened to him. It's true that when you find that secret place, when you find that intimate peace when you find the great love of God and how important you are to him. It makes everything better, your perspective changes, your mind changes, your thoughts change, You begin to discover who Jesus really is when more intimate with him.

Have you ever thought about what the word "intimate" mean, it means, "close, private or personal". That's why your mind is to be totally focused on God. When you have that intimacy with him, you will be able to receive all that he has in store for you. Your thought process and wanting to be intimate with the one that created you, means, you have to elevate your faith, elevate your belief in him, elevate your thoughts of who you are, and know that you are a child of God. And he will always love you, whether you do good things or bad things but most of all, his love will never fail and never stop.

Let me share with you the experience of my intimate relationship with God. When I first lost my eyesight, I cried, I got angry, but I never thought why did this happen to me. I know there's a rationale for everything but my goal was to come to him, so that he could bring peace, understanding, and guidance to my life in this moment of great confusion.. To hold me as tight as he could, to tell me everything is going to be OK. My state of mind was fractured, what or where is my faith, my hope, and my desire? With all those emotions going on inside of me, it allowed me to let go, it allowed me to be able to experience his trust/.I found love, I found appreciation of who I am and who God is. Now I know he cries with me when I suffer. I know he feels me, when I am angry and I know he feels me, when I'm sad.

Then I think about his love for me, his willingness to be with me during a hard and difficult time in my life. These are the times when you really need that secret place, thet quiet place, that allows you to let it all out and know that you are not alone and that you are being heard. With him, I know my journey is not over, with God in my life I know that the journey that I'm on, is to draw me closer to him and to be in his presence.

So I ask you this question, **"what is stopping you from being in his presence?"** If you want to know God, his truth and his desire for your life, you have to look for him, you have to be willing to search him out, to seek him. And when you find him, you will know that you are loved so much and that your life has a meaning and a purpose. Then once you get there, know that it's about all the great things he has done for you, the things he's doing for you right now and the things he will do for you in the future. Things that he can only do through your trust, faith, and hope, but the greatest of these is love. God loves you and will never stop loving you. But first, you must learn to love yourself, because Gods loves you, everything will be OK.

My time with him, my emotions are expose, my thoughts are focused on him, the words that come out of my mouth are in praise of him and him alone. His love is not only for me, but it's for everyone, so find that intimate place, that place where you can call your own, the place where only you and God can meet and help you through those difficult times, not only through the good times, but the bad times as well. Trust him, extend your life longer by making him an intricate part of your life. Don't let the distraction get you, let God complete you, let God be your shield, let God be your step, let God be your support, so that he can help you and guide and direct your life in a way that you could never imagine.

"No matter where I am, no matter where I go, but Lord let me always be, 'IN YOUR PRESENCE".

www.ingramcontent.com/pod-product-compliance
Lightning Source LLC
Chambersburg PA
CBHW031127160726
47989CB00016B/1861